DEAR CHARLIE

*An inspirational true story of a single mother and her ability
to live a productive life with stage IV Cancer (CHARLIE).*

Jean Chynoweth

authorHOUSE®

AuthorHouse™
1663 Liberty Drive
Bloomington, IN 47403
www.authorhouse.com
Phone: 1 (800) 839-8640

Published by AuthorHouse 02/29/2020

ISBN: 978-1-7283-4738-7 (sc)
ISBN: 978-1-7283-4742-4 (e)

Print information available on the last page.

This book is printed on acid-free paper.

About This Book

This book is about sharing my story in hopes to **inspire you** in some way to have the courage and desire to live longer so you can do what you want most in your life. I won't tell you it's not difficult. I will tell I have been through more than a person should have to go through.

Dedication

I wish to dedicate this book to my Mom, Sally Ann Bott and my Aunt, Judy (Bott) Floate, whom both passed from CHARLIE during my Journey. Never does a day go by that I do not think of you! I will see you on the other side!

I wish to also dedicate this book to anyone who has had CHARLIE, who does have CHARLIE, who will have CHARLIE or who has a loved one with CHARLIE. I wish to thank my amazing team of doctors, my family and my friends for helping me through my Journey thus far. May God be with all of you and he has for all of me.

Special Thanks to my Children; Jenn & Eddie, Ellie & Derek & to my Son Connor and Dog Gus (who lived my Journey every single day). The loves of my life; Cameron, Kendell, and Harper (my grand daughters), and to David for always being there for Connor & me.

I wish to thank my amazing Team of Doctors – Dr. Great (Oncologist), Dr. G (1st Lung Surgeon), Dr. Awesome (2nd Lung Surgeon), Dr. H (Radiatiologist) and my amazing Primary Care Doctor "Dr. Keeps Me Well".

Special thanks to my new Buddy whom made this all possible for me to share my story.

Prologue

I was a healthy 49-year-old woman who was barely ever sick in her life. I was a single mother (of 3) most of my life. I was always working and taking care of my kids. Prior to and during my Journey I took on a couple neighbor boys Mitchell and Ryan and other adopted sons. It wasn't easy, but I found if I had a routine every day, it was much easier. I got up at 5:30 every morning, showered, and started the breakfast. My kids didn't eat cereal, they had a complete breakfast every morning consisting of meat, potatoes, eggs, and Milk/Juice. Sometimes I would surprise them with breakfast pizza or bacon burritos. They're favorite.

After breakfast, I took them to their respective schools. They went to 3 different schools, Highschool (9th-12th), Pathfinder (5th-6th), and Navigator (7th-8th). All within 2 miles from my house.

Breakfast meant a lot to me. This was my time to find out what's going on with them and school. No cell phones were allowed EVER during meals. As a mom, you find out a lot if you keep your lips closed and ears open. I would ask a lot of open-ended questions. I found it amazing how much they gossiped. I thought girls gossiped a lot. Not anymore, they told about everything and everyone. It was quite funny but very interesting. No.... I didn't go blabbing to their parents, I just listened. I was trying to build trust with them so they would know they could come to me for or about anything, But, make no mistake, I would have if I thought one of them would or could be in danger. As time went on, the more I knew about what was going on in school and outside of school. As a parent, especially a single parent understanding what's going on is critical to making sure they are safe and out of trouble. I took every advantage of that.

You may be wondering why I'm sharing these things in a book about "Charlie", I want you to understand what I lost and how I managed all of this. Please enjoy the ride, I will get to the point soon.

A Couple Of Important Things First:

- *If you experience frequent pain in your chest (either side), please see a Doctor. Don't pass it off as STRESS. Maybe it IS, but maybe it ISN'T.*
- *Adopt a moto to live by. Mine was "refuse to lose", yours can be whatever works for you.*

Introduction

This story is being written to help inspire others who have CHARLIE or have a relative or friend with this Disease.

My name is Jean, I was blessed to have Charlie in my life since May 11, 2012. Who is "Charlie"? Charlie is Stage IV Lung Cancer. I gave it a name because it makes people uncomfortable when you use the word Cancer. I gave it a male name because it seemed to me at the time all the men in my life had hurt me in some way. I say I was blessed to have CHARLIE because I believe I am. It's allowed me to see the best in people, and in myself through this journey. I do not know if I could have gotten through to this point without my friends and family. My outlook has most definitely changed since that diagnosis in 2012.

Before The Diagnosis 2011

I had been getting pains in my chest for over 2 years. But I assumed they were stress related. The company I worked for at the time was preparing to be sold. This meant reductions in workforce in order to remain profitable and attract the best buyer. This also included reducing my own department (Human Resources). Maybe Management will one day understand if the company is going up **or** down, HR workloads always increase.

I was responsible for all due diligence requests relating to HR from prospective buyers and ultimately, responsible for closing our company and re-opening our new company.

This meant close and reopen everything HR related (terminating and rehiring all Colleagues, hourly & salaried, All new handbooks, benefits, training, health & safety, 401k, etc. This was a big job with now 2 of us (Stacey and myself) for 3 buildings. I took on the Sale and she handled the HR responsibilities for the 3 facilities.

After our Grand Re-opening we (The Executive Team) traveled to the new parent company in Germany. This was an amazing time. We stayed in Munich one day and Osnabrück a couple more days. We learned a lot and I spent all my time with my new German Boss (Frank). Two weeks after our return, Frank passed away suddenly. God bless his sole. This meant I had no Boss nor Partner from Germany. It was extremely difficult when our President/CEO was half-way out-the-door and I knew it. I was to report to Axel the Corporate President who knew nothing of US Human Resources.

You see I started the Michigan Karmann Manufacturing HR Department from the ground up (literally). I worked all the time (I even took my work to my son's football practices). All while I was having chest pains and thinking it was stress related.

As I look back, I think I was a FOOL to not go to the doctor, I MEAN REALLY?

Stacey, my co-partner and close friend continued to urge me to go to the Doctor. For some reason, I couldn't find it as important as what I was responsible for at work. PLEASE NEVER DO THAT. Looking back, the only anger I feel about CHARLIE is my own and not going to the Doctor earlier.

But I believe things happen for a reason and I also believe GOD will not give us more than we can handle. Maybe it was my calling to inspire others by my resilience in managing this disease and sharing my story so you could believe you can live a productive happy life with CHARLIE as well. Due to my President, Erik, being transferred to another position in Germany, the New President (I knew was being planted) to take his position did step into his position.

He wished to change the HR Department to be administrative only. Not something I was interested in. Very complicated situation, but ultimately, I negotiated my exit. I have and will always miss my co-workers (Stacey, Erica, Michael, Steve S, Dan, Jim B, Steve B, and all the other colleagues.)

I never got to say goodbye to the Colleagues that I loved so very much, and it was a tremendous burden on my soul.

Being A Full-Time Mom 2011

I took the summer off to be a "MOM" for my son and his friends. The very first time in my adult life I didn't work while raising my children. I had no chest pains which made me believe the pains I was having when I was working were STRESS RELATED.

I created "summer school" for them which included math, English, social studies, etc. a little competition, and fun activities like scavenger hunts, nail polish competitions. Ever see boys having a nail polish competition? It was HILLARIOUS! I had my phone on video in the corner, and to this day they don't believe I really did video it. Before I knew it, other friends of Connor's were asking to join.

A time I will never forget. Certainly, it's up there on the **Best Time** list.

New Job (January) 2012

Late in the year, I landed a great job for a start-up manufacturing bio-science company. I didn't know what bio-science was, let alone try to build an HR System for this type of business.

I was 6+ months into the new position at the University of Michigan. A wholly owned subsidary and first ever for-profit start-up company of the University of Michigan (MADMC).

This Company was writing a grant to develop and manufacture anti-warfare drugs. Which, by the way, no anti-warfare drug has ever been approved by the FDA. An example of an Anti-warfare drug would be like an anti-blocker for Anthrax.

I was tasked with building the HR Infrastructure and assist with the grant since I had so much manufacturing HR experience. The Team I was working with was absolutely WORLD CLASS. I loved what I was doing and was learning so much about bioscience and Human Resources aspects that were much different than automotive manufacturing.

We would often work well into the morning putting together binders with all of the information duplicated x7 times (The FDA would not allow electronic files without written documentation). We had a Team of us who built the binders in the circle room Richard Gere filmed a movie in. It was amazing and an incredible bonding experience.

I was not having pains in my chest which made me believe AGAIN the pains I had at the previous company were DEFINITELY STRESS related.

I started having pain in my knees. I mean bad, really bad, intolerable pains.

I thought for sure it was arthritis. I mentioned it to one of my Colleagues and she urged me to go to the doctor.

So.... I made an appointment to find a solution to the knee pain I was having. Check ✓

The appointment is in 1 week. I always chose the stairs verses elevators as I believed it was healthier. One day, I was on my way up the many stairs and got a stabbing, crazy hurting, menace of a pain on the right side of my chest that meant business.

I told my Colleague (who previously suggested the Dr. appointment), She insisted I call the doctor immediately. I did and got right in that day (Friday).

I went into the office, told him about the pains I was having in both of my knees and the pain I had in my chest earlier in the day! I asked him if I should have a chest x-ray. He said he was already going to suggest I have one done. I had the x-ray right then.

I was waiting in the room for him to come back. He re-entered about 20 minutes later and said he had the results but didn't know how to tell me. He went to sit down and damn near missed the chair. I almost laughed.

He said "You have a very large mass in your right lung" the size of a baseball. I said to the Doctor "what does that mean?"

I've always been a "give it to me straight" kind of girl. He said, well, it is very likely cancer.

The Diagnosis

I was 49 years old but, on that day, I was a **SCARED 11-YEAR-OLD** crying for a reason I didn't even understand.

No one in my family had ever had Lung Cancer. I could only think it meant I would die.

So…. should I tell someone? who? I am divorced. I have 3 Children and 1 Grandchild who was almost 4. My son was 12 at the time and lived with me 100%.

He is an Athlete. We travel the Midwest every summer. Athletics all year round. I was Team Mom for his baseball, football, and basketball. I can't tell him this. My oldest daughter (Jenn) was 31 at the time and unmarried, no children, but working full time and enrolled at Northwood University to finish her degree.

I was quite close to my mother in law (Mom2) and my x-husband (Dave). My Middle daughter (Ellie) wouldn't be able to handle this information. My only granddaughter (Cam) needed me in her life.

Who To Tell & The Scan Results?

I chose to tell my oldest daughter (Jenn) and mother-in-law (Mom2) who went with me for the CT Scan that Sunday (2 days after Dr. appt). I told no one else. I didn't want my family to worry if there was the chance it wasn't CHARLIE. Even though in my mind, the chances of that were probably very slim.

My job was going great. We were getting great feedback. It was down to us and 1 other company. Then I got the call I dreaded I would get. My doctor called and said they believed it was in-fact cancer based on the results of the scan. She scheduled a biopsy for the following day.

A couple days later I got another call from my doctor confirming it was Adenocarcinoma Lung Cancer (NSCLC – Non-Small Cell Lung Cancer).

I can't believe I find out this information on the phone and while I was at work. I took the call in a private small conference room. I cried for a time, not sure what to say, if anything. I got myself together emotionally, and went directly to my boss.

With tears still falling, I shared the news with him. I do not remember what I said, but he was amazing. Writing this now, all that seems like a lot.

I told my Boss and he told me "he would accommodate "whatever I needed". I continued to work while we were figuring out the game plan. He allowed me to take the time I needed.

Losing My Job (Again)

He called the team into a meeting a couple weeks later with ice cream. Typically, treats meant good news.

We were certain we received the Grant (Ice cream for bad news? No way!).

NOPE! He told us we did NOT receive the grant and we had 2 weeks to put our work in boxes and create a journal of what we have achieved and our electronic files on a stick.

AWESOME, I just found out I had CHARLIE and now I have no job, no insurance, no money to pay my bills and travel the Midwest with my son's basketball team. What am I going to do?

I already took a huge pay cut, the job I held prior was nearly six figures, this one was half of that. My new "I HAVE NO JOB" was ZERO. How do I do this and what do I do?

Telling My Family

I now needed to tell my family. I asked them to my house and gave them the information. It was not easy. I wasn't able to tell them without crying. I was not strong for them as I should have been. The girls cried and asked a question or two, but not many. None of us even knew what to ask. All of us were scared and somewhat angry. Connor wasn't there as he was in practice. We agreed we would hit this one day at a time. None of us really knew what this meant to our family or me.

A few days later, I went to pick Connor up at school (he was sitting with Cody, his best friend). They were both sitting on the bench just outside the school doors. I told them both because they would otherwise hear it somehow. Cody was basically part of our family and I was very good friends with his mom and dad. Neither asked any questions nor seemed to have a hard time with it. AWESOME, I THINK.

I have said during this entire Journey Connor's "business as usual expectation" kept me going and maybe even alive.

The Journey Begins

And the journey begins..... I was referred to an Oncologist.

We (Dave and I) went to the Oncologist appointment, who went over the scan with us and was telling us different options and timing. **"I" noticed something similar, but much smaller in the other lung and asked him about it. He said, "it is nothing".** Don't worry about it. We didn't buy that.

I do not recall who we asked for a referral to a Lung Surgeon, but we got one. An amazing one by reputation. The Lung Surgeon (Doctor G) reviewed the scan and agreed, **it WAS something.** He wouldn't consider surgery until he found out if this spot in my other lung was cancer as well. **Could I have Stage IV Cancer that has already metastasized?** Could it be 2 different cancers and both could mastasize?

New Focus

He set me up an appointment on Sunday for a PET SCAN. It was confirmed as cancer. Another biopsy and port insertion (a port is a direct connect to the blood stream). For those who have many treatments it's much easier than destroying your veins. I NO LONGER HAVE A SURGICAL OPTION. Knowing what I know now, Dr. G may have been the Doctor who saved my life. If they did nothing and it was a metastasis, the surgery would have been for nothing. If it was another primary, both could metastasize. It's bad enough that they chose not to radiate the one on the left, which is the one which metastasized.

Game Plan

We fired the first Oncologist (Doctor "I don't care"). Dave insisted on being my CHARLIE MANAGER (I was very grateful).

Dave went to the Cancer Center and said, "**he wasn't leaving until he gets some action and answers**". He explained the situation. He walked out of there with an awesome Nurse Navigator (Karen) and new knowledgeable, caring Oncologist for me (Dr. Great). He just happened to be the Director of Oncology.

Dr. Great was so amazing and super handsome for his age. He was the answer to my dreams of an Oncologist. Karen, my Nurse Navigator and I became very good friends. She was absolutely the BEST Nurse I've ever had and ever will have. She did say once that I was her most frequent caller (ha ha).

Dave may have saved my life by making a stand and getting the action and answers we needed.

I will forever be grateful for the courage and determination Dave displayed that day.

The Beginnings

Chemo Class, Biopsies, Radiation Planning, Chemo, Radiation, Scans, Dr. visits, etc.

I was talking to myself, GOD, my Dog (Gus) and did some pretty silly things. Ever hear of the Green Mile movie? In the movie a Large Black man was accused of raping and killing 2 small girls but he was really trying to save them. He had a super power of some kind. He would touch someone and take on their disease, anger, truths, etc. then he would open his mouth and it would go into the universe. I did that more times than you can imagine, I Don't know why, but I wasn't afraid to try any and everything that I found or thought of.

First Step Chemo/Radiation. Months of it. Not once a week, not 3 times a week, but every damn day from 9am – 3:30pm Monday – Friday. They don't treat cancer on the weekends.

Every-Day Routine: radiation first/then Chemo. The treatment center was amazing. There were 10 separate cubicles each with a layback chair, TV and a clear view of the beautiful outside patio. Most often I got my pick because I was a frequent flyer. My doctor kept telling me to be prepared to lose my hair (due to the strength of the Chemo), and I would always tell him NO I would not, and I did not. I told my friends at football practice that if I did, I was the lucky one because I had a chance at new hair and not old parched hair.

Amazing Family & Friends

My family and friends brought food every day. MOM2 kept track of these and stayed with me for quite some time. **I DIDN'T' EVEN CHARGE HER RENT!** My Aunt Jo also played a big part in helping me at home. Ellie would bring Cam over now and then.

In July of 2012 – My son is in Football practice every day, so I get home from treatments take a small nap and get him to practice. My neighbor (Rod) helped us out a lot too since his boys were also practicing at the same place/time. Every day was different for me. I started walking that summer 1-3 miles per day as much and as often as I could.

MOM GETS CHARLIE (SAME)

My mom was diagnosed with the same cancer in September. I was not able to help with her care physically because I had my own treatments going on. My Aunt Jo took care of her for the most part.

My mom had a resection of her left Lung in November 2012, The Doctor indicated the resection did not have good margins and there may be some residual cancer near her lymph nodes. She would need chemo/radiation to get the rest of the cancer. She pretended she would do this, but ultimately, never did.

Middle Daughter Gets Married

My daughter Danielle (Ellie) was married to an amazing man, Derek in September. Cameron is now 4.

My treatments continued through November of 2012. In my spare time I attended my son's football games.

Giving Thanks

I hosted Thanksgiving that year and my whole family came. I had made a video of my progress with pictures and music. I started the video out with the Song "The Climb" with flash shots of all my chemo/radiation treatments and pictures showing the progress I had made. My mom suddenly left the room, but we continued. After that, we went outside and sent up hot air balloons together as a family.

Aunt Is Diagnosed With Charlie

December was all about the holidays and family. Except: We got word that my Mothers Sister, Aunt Judy, was also diagnosed with Lung Cancer. I am still in disbelief about all of this. **In a matter of 6 months all three of us were diagnosed with Lung Cancer.**

Saturday Football Games (Home)

Every Friday night prior to home games, during Football season I would make a banner with all the players names and numbers on it so they could run through it at the start of every game. I finally smartened up a year later and made one out of material instead of using paper.

I cut it in two pieces and sewed Velcro in the middle, so I didn't have to make them every week. It really **didn't** have the same effect, but it was one that would hold a lot of memories.

I thought about sewing it together to see how that played out, but honestly, this was a big deal for the players, so I didn't do that. Connor has half the banner and I gave the other half to Nolan because he was injured, and the players all wrote something on the back of it in his honor.

Benefit & Tackle-Athon

Because I had no job, no source of income, my sons football team put together a benefit and tackle-a-thon. This was all suggested and initiated by the Youth Football Director (Our Varsity Coach Rob). My friend Jill pretty much organized the whole event.

Many of the community businesses donated merchandise and gift cards and all the youth football teams kept track of their tackles and solicited donations from their family and friends totaling $8,000 for my son and me. The benefit was held at the first game of the season which provided more than $20,000.

We all wore Red T-shirts. My whole family was there and many of my friends. The Channel 7 sports anchor came to one of the practices and video-taped us and it was on the local news.

I never missed a game and I video-taped all his games with my Granddaughter Cam sitting right by my side.

My sister Tina had a benefit that raised over $8,000, I cannot explain how amazing and humbling all of this was for me. They literally allowed us to continue living in our house and remaining "as we were".

There Is Nothing Clinical About This Trial

My scans were showing very little progress, so my Doctor suggested I attend a clinical trial. The Trial was at Karmanos in Detroit about 1+ hour from my house. The Trial started in December 2012. I had more biopsy's done. I asked if the sheets were washed as the surgical pre-op area was a mess and didn't appear very sterile. It was not a very classy facility. I would not recommend this facility to anyone.

My Aunt Jo took me almost every time. My lung tumors increased and did not decrease so we ended the trial on March 25th. I made a friend there who's sister prepared me for my radiation treatments daily. We met a couple times for lunch but then in time we stopped meeting.

Charlie Is Dancing

I started this new year out WITH A BANG! On January 3rd, 2013– I found out I had 3 tumors on my brain. My Options were to radiate the tumors or whole brain radiation. I chose the ladder because it had a higher chance of it not returning. Although whole brain radiation would cause much worse short term memory loss. A total of 15 treatments, every day for 3 weeks. I believe this was the most fatigue I have endured since the start.

Getting Warm

Mom2 and Dad invited me to Florida for a couple weeks to recuperate in warm temperatures, sleep as much as needed and a safe place to walk as much as I could. I arrived on my Mom2's 72nd birthday (February 7th, 2013). It was a surprise and she was thrilled. I sure hope they know how much I love them and how much I appreciate them taking me in as their "daughter". I'm still struggling with short term memory issues, but I always find my way. There was a short time where I couldn't complete a sentence, stuttered once in a while, but that also got better over time. When I returned, I had an amazing updated Kitchen all done by Eddie, my son-in-law and it was Fantastik.

As I age, it's tough to know what's caused by the treatments and what is simply aging. I think I'll continue to blame it on treatment. It's easier and makes me feel better. I tried to tell my Doctor I wasn't going to lose my hair (it had worked so far) but he said when your radiation is going through your scalp, there is no chance to keep your hair.

Where Is My Hair?

I had a hair buzzing party complete with Budweiser Light. My daughters took turns cutting and shaving my head. I had already prepared for this day and had bought a couple of wigs. It was fun and funny. Cam, my granddaughter asked a lot of questions. Connor wanted no part of it. The funny thing that happened was I had no hair when Cam went downstairs to play with Connor and when she came upstairs, I had one of the wigs on and **she said "Grandma, your hair grew back already?" all serious. We all laughed**.

Kendall Rae – 2Nd Granddaughter

My 2nd Granddaughter, Boo-Boo (Kendall Rae) was born on March 10, 2013. I was there during her birth and video-taped as much as they would allow. How amazing that was. Her and I still have a special bond to this day.

Aunt Passes

Aunt Judy (Moms Sister) passed on March 15th. I was able to see her prior to her death which I am grateful for to this day. She called me when I was in Florida earlier in the year to talk to me about her cancer and my thoughts on smoking. I told her to do what she felt most comfortable with (we talked for 2 hours).

In the meantime, Mom2 was driving around the sub-division looking for me and found me sitting on a bench. What she didn't know was I was smoking. She was worried, I was not! I got in the van with her to go back and shared my Aunt's call with her.

When the Cancer went to my brain, I was certainly going to die so I started smoking again. I felt sick to my stomach the first puff. ashamed of myself so I threw it out the window, I was so guilt ridden. 10 minutes later I got out another and smoked only half. When and since I started smoking again, it has caused me even more grief. I now was in hiding from everyone, finding ways to be alone or drive so I could smoke. You may ask why would I do this? Addiction is the only answer. I (again) couldn't put my own life ahead of something more important (like the stress I had prior to Charlie, only much worse). I feel terrible about it, I've asked GOD to help me a thousand times, My son gave me a very lovingly lecture one evening, I ran into my room crying and I called 1-800-Quit and asked for help. I feel ashamed with every puff I take even to this day.

They sent me patches which I didn't find helpful. This added to my stress and I felt so much guilt and shame. But I still couldn't do it. It is on my bucket list and hopefully one day soon God will help me get this into my thick skull and just do it. Until then, I continue to hide it as much as I can and feel terribly guilty about it.

My Son Connor had his first TEENAGE BIRTHDAY (13). Can't wait for all the things to come.....

Charlie Will Not Listen To Me

I'm back in Chemo on April 7, 2013. I spent my 50th birthday in section 10 at the Cancer Center. I was surprised by my kids/granddaughter, Dave and Mom2 and Dad. They all came in with a "lit up" birthday cake. This was against the infusion center "LAWS", but they made an exception for me.

My family and friends threw me a "50th" Birthday party with an 80's theme. My daughters AND my sister (Tina) had everything for me to change into. It was a fantastic night!

Anonymous Birthday Surprises

30 days prior to this party, I started getting birthday surprises on my door step every day. They were always "anonymous". My friend Julie had organized this entire thing and made a book of this she gave me at my party.

Maggie's

I started working part time at an organic vegetable farm called "Maggie's" In the spring of 2013. It was located about two miles from my home.

Maggie's was like a co-op; the members did the work and got their vegetables for free. Julie and Mom2 both came with me each once to see what it was like. I went there once a week and weeded, washed vegetables, or bagged up the vegetables.

Other Events

Connor joined the track team. He wasn't very good and didn't like it. I went to a couple of his meets and volunteered to "time" one or two of the events. Otherwise, I would be standing around waiting for paint to dry. As you can see Mom isn't a fan either. I felt it would enhance his leg strength and benefit him in football and basketball. He later quit baseball due to a conflict with basketball practice.

Daughter Graduates College

My daughter Jenn graduated from Northwood University on Saturday, May 11th, 2013, the anniversary of my diagnosis. Ironic isn't it?

Hello Tarciva

No-go with this last Chemo nor the Clinical Trial so here comes Tarciva. a Chemo pill newly approved. I began taking it on the 30th of July.

Volunteering

I started volunteering at the cancer center where I had my chemo. That was my way of giving back. It was great while it lasted but I stopped going and don't remember why.

New Year New Treatments 2014

Scans show progression in my lungs so back on radiation/chemo daily routine. During this time, Mom2 & Dad stayed at my house. Dad remodeled the basement all in school colors so Connor could have his friends over and leave me alone (ha-ha). It was just a plain basement with carpet and a large TV.

He built a wall with a door so the storage and furnace area would be hidden and put a door where the washer and dryer were located. Dad and Mom2 painted it gray and red (school colors).

Dad also put a door around the fuse box with a secret trap inside where I could put my safe. I never told anyone until I sold the house. The basement turned out amazing. This man can do anything.

Settle Down Galbladder

I started having horrendous stomach pain at the treatment center while getting chemo. I was crying, curled up like a newborn and not understanding why. **Amazing.. it's my Gallbladder talking to me**. **Hello?** They gave me morphine to take the pain away. They wouldn't let me have surgery to remove it until I was done with Chemo/radiation. They sent me home with a bottle of liquid morphine. **Really?** I didn't even know morphine could be given to a patient to take home. It was scary and comforting at the same time.

Last day chemo/radiation May 27th. 2014 This was a big day for me and my family.

Janice, my most favorite Nurse at the Chemo Center and I rang the bell and danced out the door. She's since left for Texas. **I HAVE NOT NOR WILL EVER HAVE CHEMO AGAIN. ALL DONE WITH THAT!** Gallbladder Surgery June 9, 2014

Jenn Is Engaged

I never thought I would see this day! She says Eddie took her to dinner. After dinner, they got into their truck. Eddie wasn't leaving or saying anything. Apparently, Jenn said, "why are we not leaving" and he pops out the ring and gives it to her. How romantic (LOL). Who cares, he may not have the gift of romantic gestures, but he is a good man and very much like Jenn.

My Mom Passes

Mom spent the last 6 months of her life in a hospice home which was beautiful. When she got bad in June of 2014, I stayed with her as much as I could, as did Aunt Jo.

I stayed in a chair next to her bed on the night of July 4, 2014. She was angry with me the night before because I cried so much, and she yelled at me.... **Jean Ann..... that's enough!** It was at that moment I said ok mom, you can go if you want, but I want you to know how much I love you and how grateful I am for all you have done for me.

As I laid beside her in my chair pushed up next to her bed I couldn't sleep, just closed my eyes and opened them to see that she was breathing. There were fireworks going off well beyond midnight and I had a feeling she would leave me that night, so I just kept watching to see if she was breathing.

My Aunt Jo (Moms only remaining Sister) was down the hall laying/sleeping on a couch. I turned toward the window about 6 am and seriously minutes later the nurse and my aunt came in and they said, "she's gone". I said "NO" that can't be, I just turned over a few minutes ago and she was breathing.

I climbed in bed with her, placed her arm around me and wouldn't leave until they finally pulled me off her.

I think by then my brother and sister and rest of the family had arrived and wanted to say good-bye to her. **This was one of**

the most difficult of days I have ever endured in my whole life.

We had a very nice service for her. She touched the lives of so many and endured so much pain since the passing of my father in 1969. I was 6, my brother 7, and my sister 4. In an instant she was a widow with 3 children, no job, no anything. She struggled her whole life and I believe she couldn't get past Dad's death. She some how found a way to help others early on, many of our childhood friends remained in touch with her. Standing room only at the funeral. I was happy for her that she knew she had touched so many lives in a positive way.

All About Basketball 2015

It's now all about basketball, traveling with school team and AAU Team. Connor is down to 1 sport, but that one sport keeps us traveling all year round. I loved every minute of it though! I've video-taped most of his games, but videotaping was getting old.

Charlie Is Moving Again

CHARLIE has been quite busy this year. He decided to land in my back bones, specifically the Sacrum section of my lower back. No Chemo, Just Radiation. This was the only event in 2015 for CHARLIE. Dr. Great always made sure I was free from treatments during the holidays and this year was no exception.

Oldest Daughter Jenn Married 2015

JENN and EDDIE were married in September of 2015. She was a planner by-day, so the reception was held at her workplace. In this beautiful building in north town. Everything was Amazing. She is the only one I know that can pull something like this off nearly by herself.

Charlie Is Busy, Busy, Busy 2016

CHARLIE has been quite busy again this year, going into my adrenal gland this time. If you recall or not, the Pituitary gland in your brain sends hormones to the adrenal glands to manage the fight or flight of your hormones, among other things.

During this period, I was very unstable. I was either angry for no reason or every reason or I cried for no reason or every reason. However, I was able to select Cyber Knife (very pinpointed version of radiation), very high dose, very high fatigue. 5 times was all. I was not allowed to drive so 4 family members and 1 friend each took me once. They lasted about an hour each.

Harper Quinn (3Rd Granddaughter)

Harper is the mini-me of Jenn, so beautiful. Harper was born on July 25th of this year (2016)

The rest of the year was pretty much uneventful. My son is now 16 and is getting really good at Basketball. He also has his Driver's license, watch out world! He was in the paper a couple of times and was listed as one of the top 5 in our county.

Charlie Is Content 2017

CHARLIE must be quite content or non-existent the rest of 2017. I continue to get scans every 3 months, but no CHARLIE detected. I get MRI's every 6 months just to assure he hasn't returned. The rest of 2017 was full of odd details like looking for a job, going to sports events, Team Mom duties, traveling the Midwest, birthday parties and rest when I needed it.

Introducing Chuck, Charlie's Cousin

In January OF 2018, CHARLIE's cousin CHUCK" came to the party and landed in my right lung. He was a new Primary Cancer. He was much smaller than Charlie, but trouble none-the-less.

We consulted and discussed my options with Dr. Great and Dr. New Lung Surgeon (The Lung Cancer Team all met earlier as they normally do each Tuesday). They all agreed I could have Surgery or Cyber Knife. **My first ever opportunity for surgery they said I could never have**. I was Surgery all the way. Dave was Cyber knife all the way. His concerns were if they opened me up, it would spread. My Surgeon said flat out NO, it would not. The result, I get to have surgery for the first time because of my resilience during the past years. I was just getting to the point I didn't need a nap every day. Surgery it is. I was scheduled the following week.

They took it out and I was home in 2 or 3 days. My only visitor was my friend Jeffey. We walked and talked. Great recovery!

Spring Break 2018

Two weeks after Surgery, we were on our way to Florida for a 7-day cruise to the Caribbean. My son and I had historically always gone on some vacation during Spring Break. This was our last one as he was graduating this June.

His girlfriend and my friend Chris went with us. All 4 of us in one room. We had a great time. Cave Tubing was my favorite event, but very tough after only being out of surgery a couple weeks. The guides helped me across all the rocky streams and up the hills. The Caves were Magnificent. I wish I had a camera because at one point there was a break in the cave, and we saw PARIDISE. I'm not kidding, it was so beautiful it could very well be Paradise.

We returned home had a super great time. Now, get ready for his Graduation. He had already signed to play basketball for Dominican University near Chicago.

They held this in the Gym at his High School. Lots of Pics with family and friends.

Graduation For Connor

Everything went GREAT, I was preparing the house, yard, garage all summer in preparation. During this time, I got a call from Scottie, my stepson, about selling my house. I intended to put it on the market after graduation. The buyers really wanted a house in our subdivision and wanted to see it today.

I said ok but it was being torn apart as I was getting ready for a party (painting, moldings, etc.). I left while it was being shown.

I got a call from Scottie about 20 minutes later. He said "Sold" for asking price. WOW! Sold without even putting it on the market.

Graduation party was a great time for all. Connor was very happy with the turnout as was I. So now, let's get packed up for you to go to your dorm at Dominican and me to move to an apartment. No need for a big house and yard.

Big Move Into Apartment Living

At the end of July 2018, we moved some of the big stuff into the apartment such as beds, etc. Connor and I stayed in the Apartment that night. Our first night NOT in our house. I found myself overwhelmed. I no longer have a house, my son is about to go 6.5 hours away to play ball at Dominican University in Chicago. I don't know how I'm going to put a house into an apartment. Every aspect of my life is now different or has disappeared. Loneliness is not my strong suit. You spend your whole life giving and doing and one day it is gone-with-the wind.

I got up the next morning throwing up blood. A lot of blood. Cups of blood. I reacted fast, got dressed and I drove to the emergency room because I knew it would take longer for an ambulance and was quite lucid and felt I could drive.

I recorded the time of arrival in the book I keep in my purse. I also recorded the Dr and Nurses names. That's the last I remember.

I was in **an induced coma** for 3 days while they searched for the bleeders. Of course, my kids and family were all there during this time (I don't recall of course). Tina stayed in my room, slept in my room the whole time I was in the Coma. Apparently, I continued to tell her she was not my sister, but infact, an imposter.

Ellie was the only one I would allow to suction me. I was in and out of crankiness the whole time.

The Doctor discovered the bleeders were from my right lung. Because of the amount of radiation I had had over the years, the blood vessels were regenerating and were small. They suspect I lifted a heavy object or ran into something during the move the day prior. We will never know the answer to that.

Coming Home (To A New Apartment)

I came home on the 6th day. OMG! My daughters, Jenn and Ellie (I'm not sure if others helped). I assume they did. When I got home, the apartment was all set up with most of my belongings. Jenn even bought new bathroom towels and rugs to make it seem like home. My granddaughter Cam organized my kitchen.

What an amazing family I have. For them to do this for me was like a dream come true. Except, WHO MOVED MY CHEESE? I'm still looking for things I hope got moved.

Dominican, Here Comes Connor

I wasn't allowed to drive so my daughter Ellie drove me and my son to his First College 2 or 3 days after I returned home.

Move & Move Again

I have moved to a bottom floor since I have a 15-year-old German Short Hair. This allows me no stairs for which never liked me anyway. I took 2 big falls for which one of them was all the way down on cement stairs, brusised my ribs, slight concussion, but the worst part was tearing my favorite Jeans. I had an emergency tech who lived upstairs take a peek at me, but I ended up at the Dr's. Later that week, I requested a lock per the housing Act of somewhere. This way the patio door is my primary entry and exit. I've made a Beautiful friend since I've moved downstairs, her name is Gail and I have been blessed to live right by her.

I've been asked to speak about my story several times, but I am not a fan of public speaking, in-fact, I think I turn every shade of blue there is. I did agree to speaking at the Lung Cancer Vigil my hospital has every year.

I spoke Once. I was most certainly purple, if it wasn't for my grand-daughter (Cam), I wouldn't have been able to do it. I put together my story on video so between Cam and the video screen I made my message clear. YOU CAN LIVE WITH LUNG CANCER.

If I have said this once, twice, or many times. I am living PROOF that YOU CAN LIVE WITH CHARLIE!!!

I Bless you with this message:

Never Give in or Give up. Your life is as beautiful as you are. Good things will Happen for you during this process.

I have a large plague in my kitchen, it reads:
**"*GOOD MORNING, THIS IS GOD, I WILL BE*
HANDLING ALL YOUR PROBLEMS TODAY!
*May God Bless You as he has Me***

Written by Jean (Oliver) Chynoweth

Lung Cancer False Beliefs

#1-Smokers Only Get Lung Cancer Actually, many people that develop lung cancer are non or x-smokers. Ten percent of people overall, and 20% of women with lung cancer are non-smokers.

#2-There is Nothing I Can Do to Lower My Risk of Lung Cancer Indeed avoiding smoking can lower your risk of developing lung cancer, but an awareness of other factors that may raise or lower your risk is helpful as well. Some environmental exposures such as radon can raise your risk, and occupational exposures account for 13% to 29% of lung cancers in men. On the bright side, a healthy diet and exercise appear to lower risk.

#3-Lung Cancer Rates Are Declining Now That Fewer People Smoke This may be true or false. From 1991 to 2005, lung cancer rates decreased approximately 1.8% per year among men, and increased 0.5% per year among women.

#4-Living in a Polluted environment is a Greater Risk Than Smoking Being exposed to diesel exhausts and air pollution does raise the risk of lung cancer; however, the risk is minimal in comparison to smoking.

#5-If I Already Have Lung Cancer, it Doesn't Matter if I Quit Smoking There are several reasons to quit smoking after a diagnosis of lung cancer. Stopping this habit can raise the success rate of surgery, makes your treatment more effective, and lowers your risk of dying from causes other than lung cancer.

#6-I Am Too Young to Have Lung Cancer Lung cancer is more common in elderly people, but can occur in young people and even children.

#7-I Am Too Old for Treatment Your age in and of itself shouldn't determine whether a lung cancer is treated. It appears that the young at heart and positive minded people are often able to tolerate chemotherapy as well as younger people and have a similar quality of life following surgery, if offered to them. Performance status (a measure of how well a person can do ordinary daily activities) is a better indicator of how well someone will tolerate various treatments.

#8-Lung Cancer is a Death Sentence-Certainly the survival rate for lung cancer overall is not what we wish it to be. Most people are diagnosed with the disease at a stage beyond which a cure is possible. But even if a lung cancer is not curable, it is still treatable. And treatment can often not only extend your life, but it can help lessen some of the symptoms of CHARLIE as well. I am proof of all of these False Beliefs.

Personal Suggestions (Based On My Experiences)

1. Do not jump on the computer and type in Lung Cancer after a diagnosis. Please remember these are paid advertisers. If you want to learn more about your cancer, ask your doctor. If you must, go to a reputable facility online such as the Mayo Clinic, MD Anderson, CCOA.

2. Do not assume the worst. We typically react this way with the un-known, but I advise you to take it one step at a time, one day at a time and learn as much as you can. Knowledge is a blessing not a curse. The wrong knowledge is a curse.

3. The most **important thing** in this fight is **YOUR ATTITUDE**. You must stay positive and **refuse to lose.**

4. You want the best Oncologist you can find ask your family and friends. It's perfectly ok to ask for referrals on social media as well. This is your life!

5. Always have one person with you at all appointments to take notes. Prepare for each appointment with questions. Keep a Journal. You will always be inclined to review your notes.

6. Find one person whom you can talk to openly and freely without judgement. I live alone and sometimes I just let

my dog have it all. He is truly the best listener. I've always said "Everyone needs an Aunt Jo", She has always been there to listen and ask questions without judgement. This is a very important step not to miss or you will carry the burden alone inside and that's never good. **Don't keep it all in**. I've always been the strong one in our family and sometimes, actually most of the time. I act as though everything is fine when it isn't. I don't want to let them down or think I'm not who they think I am, It's my job to be there for them "always". Then I lose it and fall on the floor crying "God.... Just take me now, I can't take any more. Or I crawl to my bed and cry. My Dog knows and is at my head or will come lay with me every single time. I'll be fine and dandy I tell him. It's ok to do this as much or as often as you need to. It helps get it out and back to "business as usual".

7. Ask for a copy of every scan and the notes provided by the person who read and interpreted them. Most radiology departments will gladly burn a cd for you. You may need it in the future if you decide to change doctors or move. I keep mine in a binder, most recent on top. I bought top loaders and would add to it if something else was mailed. It would be much faster to give your new doctor. It may also help with Insurance issues.

8. Insist on fast service. Don't be afraid to rock-the-boat. It's your boat and it's your responsibility to rock it if need be. My x-husband once had to stand in the middle of the hospital and wouldn't move until he got action.

9. You will benefit greatly by asking someone to manage your care, treatments, scans, paperwork, calendar, food, etc. If they are not available, I recommend you order your food in. Definitely ask for a Nurse Navigator if they have them. They can coordinate your doctors visits (and you will have a lot). You need to concentrate on YOU and not things others you pay can do for you.

Never Settle

Don't settle for anyone other than the "BEST" by either reputation or by talking to others (a referral). I can give you many examples of friends-of-friends of mine whom I have referred. My Oncologist is the Director of Oncology in my hospital known for their innovative cancer treatments. You may not get the Director, but you stand a better chance at getting a Dr. Great.

Insist on getting to your Oncologist appointment within 5 days of any scans or you will drive yourself crazy worrying.

Lastly, we who have Charlie tend to think every ache and pain is a new or revisited cancer.

Pay attention to your body and how you feel each day. You will sometimes know if it is or isn't if you listen to your body. (it's never 100%) I've been wrong once! My doctor has learned to believe me. It's also possible to have pains in other areas that signal Charlie is back. Mine are my knees and club fingers. Dr. Great has a word for this, but I can never remember.

Find humor in everything possible. Try your hardest to do what you did prior to the diagnosis, but again, listen to your body and rest when you need to and can.

Lastly live by the MOTO **"REFUSE TO LOSE".** Always look forward to something in the future such as your next birthday or your son's graduation or your daughter's marriage. This helps to achieve longevity.

There are many, many diets out there being presented to help with cancer. I didn't follow a specific diet I just ate healthy. No fast food, natural fruits and vegetables (I buy them frozen). Eat what you like. You don't have to eat the things you do not like; you just have to eat healthy. LIMIT your sugar intake. What they say is TRUE. CHARLIE likes to feed off sugar and reproduce.

Exercise within your limits. Start small and work up to what your body can handle. If you live in a state where there is winter, look for a station on TV or your computer. Walk around your house. You don't have to join a gym to exercise. There are many things you can do.

I am currently in an apartment, but you'd be amazed at how many times I walk back and forth, my German Short Hair follows me, it takes him about 6 times to say he quits. I also have a noise and motion activated 1 ft. palm tree. I pull it out every Christmas. When Gus my dog or I make it go off its an automatic shake-shake-shake during the whole song. Be creative with what you do to exercise, but DO exercise, it Is good for the mind AND soul, and your body will thank you.

I DO hope you got something from this book, either inspiration or an idea from my experience. My whole heart and body hope you do. It is 2020 now and I'm healthy and have no signs of CHARLIE. If I can do this, so can YOU! I am considering a move to Tennessee where it is warmer, but still drivable to come home to see my family. Walking is great for me, but you get 3-4 months in Michigan. I need to walk year-round. I am also selling products on-line to earn extra income.

MAY GOD BLESS YOU AND YOUR FAMILY.

CPSIA information can be obtained
at www.ICGtesting.com
Printed in the USA
LVHW090249130320
649960LV00001B/73